WIMBLEDON LAWN TENNIS MUSEUM

With more than 70 featured Museum scenes and objects and a host of famous tennis faces, we hope that you will find this handbook both useful as a guide and enjoyable as a souvenir of your visit.

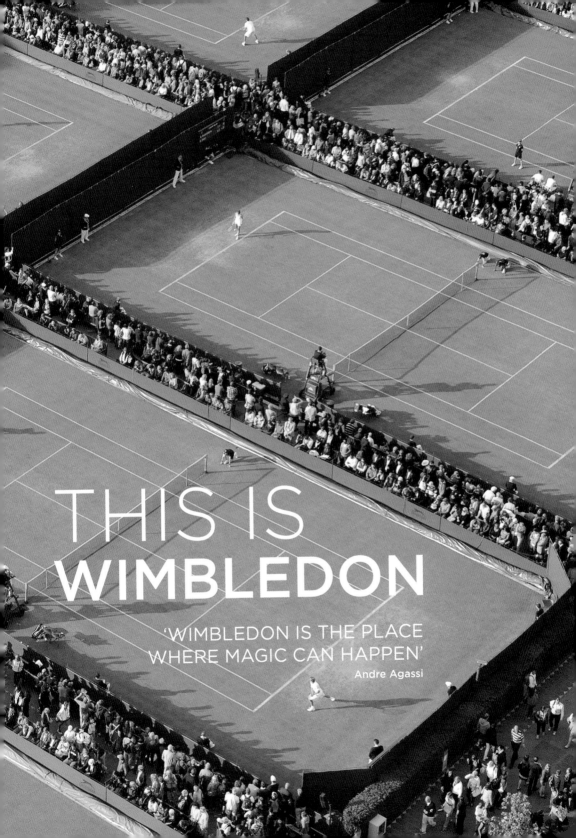

THIS IS
WIMBLEDON

'WIMBLEDON IS THE PLACE
WHERE MAGIC CAN HAPPEN'
Andre Agassi

EVERY YEAR, HUNDREDS OF THOUSANDS OF PEOPLE VISIT THE CHAMPIONSHIPS AT WIMBLEDON.

Over a billion worldwide watch on television or online. Tennis has evolved from its beginnings as a leisured pastime in Victorian England to become a dynamic, professional, global sport.

Wimbledon Lawn Tennis Museum celebrates the traditions, emotions, sights and sounds that have made Wimbledon the finest stage in world tennis. It uncovers the story of lawn tennis and the 'Fortnight'. Historic objects, interactive displays and classic Wimbledon film footage reveal significant moments ranging from the earliest days to the triumphs of the modern champions.

The Museum moved to its present location in 2006, bringing expanded space and fresh, exciting exhibits and galleries. It also houses The Kenneth Ritchie Wimbledon Library, the world's pre-eminent collection of tennis books, periodicals, videos and DVDs.

The majority of the objects, paintings, drawings and photographs documented in this handbook can be seen in the Museum.

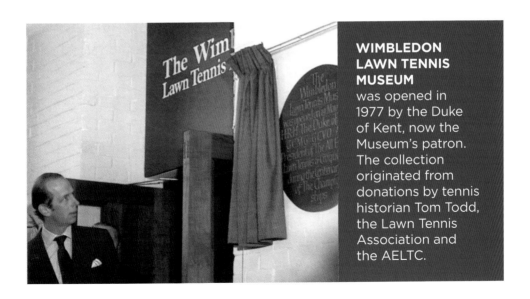

WIMBLEDON LAWN TENNIS MUSEUM was opened in 1977 by the Duke of Kent, now the Museum's patron. The collection originated from donations by tennis historian Tom Todd, the Lawn Tennis Association and the AELTC.

Previous page: Aerial view of the southern courts during The Championships, 2013
Left: Classic Kit showcase in the Museum

BEFORE
LAWN TENNIS

'TENNIS IS A PERFECT
COMBINATION OF VIOLENT
ACTION TAKING PLACE
IN AN ATMOSPHERE
OF TRANQUILITY'
Billie Jean King

MINTON

3, Army officers on leave from
visited the Duke of Beaufort's
at Badminton in Gloucestershire.
they played with lightweight
s strung with thin gut to hit a
ecock back and forth over a
et. Today, Badminton is one of
orld's most popular racket sports.

MANY GAMES WITH BATS AND BALLS WERE PLAYED BEFORE LAWN TENNIS DEVELOPED INTO A DISTINCT GAME.

Battledore, or shuttlecock, was played with a light feathered cork (the shuttlecock) and a small bat with parchment or vellum stretched tightly across the frame (the battledore). It was non-competitive, the aim being to keep the shuttlecock in the air for as long as possible. This game, well over 1,000 years old, became the badminton we recognise today.

Rackets, played with long-handled rackets and a small hard white ball, is one of the fastest sports in the world. It started in London at the debtors' prisons and, by contrast, Harrow School. The game of squash is a descendant of rackets.

Real tennis, also known as court tennis or royal tennis, had its origins in jeu de paume (game of the palm) played in the royal palaces and monastic cloisters of 12th and 13th century France. It involved hitting the ball across a net, using the hand. How jeu de paume became 'tennis' is a mystery. It might derive from the call of 'tenez' (meaning 'hold' or 'look out') which a player had to shout before serving. By the 16th century, wooden rackets strung with thick gut were being used. The balls, made of compressed hair or wool stitched inside a cloth or leather cover, had little bounce.

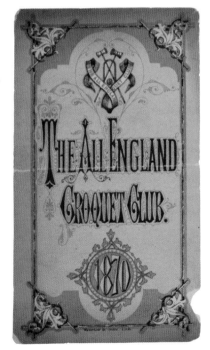

In mid-Victorian England, the main summer sport of the leisured classes was croquet. Played on the lawns of large homes, the game involved hitting balls through metal hoops with a heavy wooden mallet. Originating from a French game, croquet provided gentle exercise outdoors for young and old, making it an ideal social pastime. On 23 July 1868 the All England Croquet Club was founded at a meeting held in the offices of *The Field*, chaired by the newspaper's editor, John Walsh. The following year, the Club leased its own ground – a field off Worple Road in Wimbledon in south-west London. The history of Wimbledon had begun.

Left: Forerunners of Lawn Tennis showcase in the Museum
Above: Cover of The All England Croquet Club membership card, 1870

THE MAJOR'S
BRAINWAVE

'A NEW GAME HAS BEEN PATENTED BY MAJOR WINGFIELD, WHICH, IF WE MISTAKE NOT, WILL BECOME A NATIONAL PASTIME'

Army and Navy Gazette, 1874

MANY REAL TENNIS OR RACKETS PLAYERS WANTED AN OUTDOOR PURSUIT THAT OFFERED MORE EXERCISE THAN GENTEEL CROQUET.

In Birmingham Harry Gem and his Spanish friend Augurio Perera experimented with a game they first called Pelota and then lawn rackets. In the early 1870s they formed a lawn rackets tennis club at the then Manor House Hotel in Royal Leamington Spa in Warwickshire.

It was however a retired army officer who first commercialised the new type of game. He was Major Walter Clopton Wingfield, a man with a creative mind and boundless energy. After serving in India and China with the Dragoon Guards, Wingfield turned his inventive talents to the creation of an outdoor sport involving physical effort but without the complex rules of Real Tennis. He devised a game with an hourglass-shaped court and a high sagging net and called it Sphairistikè – an ancient Greek word that can roughly be translated as 'ball game'.

In 1874 Wingfield applied for a patent which was duly issued. He enthusiastically marketed the boxed sets of equipment for his game, which he sensibly re-named 'Sphairistikè or Lawn Tennis'. The lawns of middle-class England were transformed. With much publicity, its popularity spread throughout the world.

MEMBERS OF THE All England Croquet Club were among those caught up in the enthusiasm. At the suggestion of member Dr Henry Jones (second from left), one of its croquet lawns was set aside for the new game of lawn tennis. In 1877, the Club changed its name to The All England Croquet and Lawn Tennis Club.

Left: Major Walter Clopton Wingfield
Above from top to bottom: Sphairistikè book of rules, 1876; Members of The All England Croquet Club, 1870

THE EARLY
CHAMPIONSHIPS

'PROPOSED BY MR WALSH, SECONDED BY
MR EVELEIGH, THAT A PUBLIC MEETING BE HELD
ON JULY 10th AND FOLLOWING DAYS TO COMPETE
FOR THE CHAMPIONSHIPS IN LAWN TENNIS'

All England Club Minutes, 2 June 1877

THE DECISION TO HOLD THE WORLD'S FIRST LAWN TENNIS CHAMPIONSHIP WAS MADE ALMOST BY ACCIDENT.

In June 1877 The All England Croquet and Lawn Tennis Club adopted the suggestion of one of its members, John Walsh, to stage a competition open to all-comers. Legend has it that he suggested the competition in order to raise money for the repair of a broken pony roller, essential for the upkeep of the lawns.

A sub-committee was appointed, led by Dr Henry Jones, to draw up rules for 'a Championship'. With great foresight Jones and his team decreed that a rectangular court, 26 yards long, nine yards wide, would be used and that real tennis scoring (15, 30, 40, deuce, advantage) would be adopted rather than the '15 points up' system used in rackets. The net would be five feet high at the posts and three feet three inches at the centre. The Club's croquet lawns were set up for the tournament and Jones himself acted as referee.

THE FIRST CHAMPION, from an entry of 22 players, was Spencer Gore. Gore, who had attended Harrow School and played rackets, beat real tennis player William Marshall in the final in three straight sets. The winner's prize was a silver Challenge Cup presented by *The Field*. Some 200 spectators paid one shilling each to watch the match on a rainy afternoon, thus contributing £10 to Club funds.

Left: Drawing of the first Championship, 1877
Above from left to right: Spencer Gore; Winner's silver Challenge Cup;
Enamel box commemorating the first Championship centenary, 1977

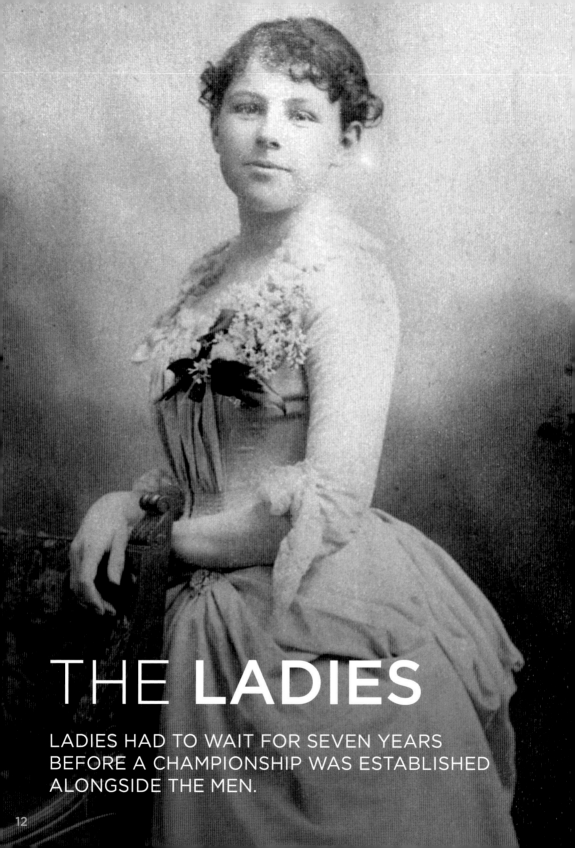

THE **LADIES**

LADIES HAD TO WAIT FOR SEVEN YEARS
BEFORE A CHAMPIONSHIP WAS ESTABLISHED
ALONGSIDE THE MEN.

It was Dr Henry Jones again who led the way. In 1884 he persuaded the Committee that a Ladies' Singles Championship should be held at the same time as the new Gentlemen's Doubles event, also due to start that year. The first Ladies' Champion was Maud Watson. From an entry of 13 players the 19-year-old from Warwickshire beat her elder sister Lilian in the final.

There was no trophy for the first two years of the Ladies' Singles event. Instead the winner and runner up were presented with money to buy their own prizes. For winning the first Championship Maud Watson chose a silver flower basket. Fifty years later Maud presented the basket to the Edgbaston Priory Club for its annual junior tournament. It is kindly loaned annually to the Museum by the Edgbaston Priory Club.

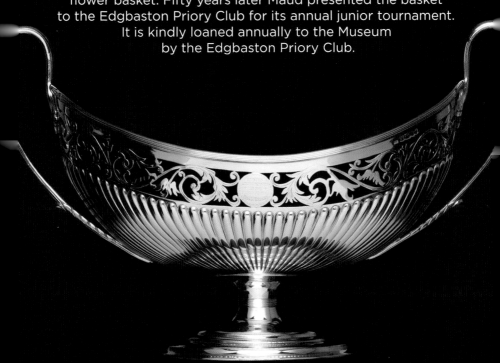

MAUD'S SISTER LILIAN chose a silver-backed hairbrush and mirror set as the second prize in 1884.

The Ladies' Singles trophy was first presented in 1886 and from then, the Ladies' Champion was also presented with a bracelet.

Left: Maud Watson, the first Ladies' Centre: Maud Watson chose a silver Championships, 1884

A VICTORIAN
CRAZE

'UNDER ANY CIRCUMSTANCES SUCH A GAME AS LAWN TENNIS WOULD NOT HAVE FAILED TO ACHIEVE POPULARITY AND SUCCESS'

Lawn Tennis: Its Players and How to Play, Lieutenant-Colonel Robert D. Osborn, 1881

LAWN TENNIS RAPIDLY BECAME A POPULAR PASTIME AND PART OF THE SOCIAL ROUND.

It gave young men and women an opportunity to meet and socialise, while enjoying a new game in the open air.

All over the country, lawn tennis clubs sprang up and started their own tournaments. Archery, croquet and badminton clubs went over to the new game and skating rinks were converted into courts. The principal growth took place in suburban locations, where tennis clubs became centres of activity for the whole family.

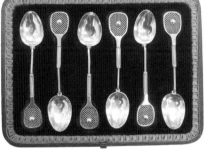

Designers and manufacturers soon picked up on the popularity of the sport and used it for decoration. The new game invaded drawing rooms, parlours, dining rooms and kitchens as nets, rackets and balls inspired domestic objects ranging from the practical to the ornate. The Victorians' love affair with tennis is reflected in the Museum's extensive collection of curios, memorabilia, books, paintings and posters devoted to the game.

Left: *The Wimbledon Tennis Party* by E.F. Brewtnall, 1891
Above from left to right: The 'Zero' ice cream maker, 1880s; a novelty thermometer, 1880s; Six silver teaspoons, 1893

THE WORPLE ROAD
YEARS

THE ALL ENGLAND CROQUET CLUB ESTABLISHED ITS FIRST GROUNDS NEAR WORPLE ROAD IN WIMBLEDON.

Members paid a subscription of one guinea each, which would be worth about £65 today. It was on the croquet lawns that the first Lawn Tennis Championship was held in 1877. Growth of the tournament was rapid. With the construction of a large Centre Court at the heart of the Worple Road grounds, crowds flocked to see the great champions of the 19th century.

The Challenge Round – a match between the title-holder and the winner of the All-Comers' Singles – decided the outcome of The Championships during this period. This meant that the reigning champion had only to play one match. The champions, as well as winners and runners-up in the All-Comers' events, continued to win prizes but no money.

By the Edwardian era the Wimbledon Fortnight was an established part of 'The Season' and spectators overflowed the ground. Overcrowding became a serious problem, especially after the First World War with the arrival of tennis superstars Suzanne Lenglen of France in 1919 and American Bill Tilden in 1920. Sited between the road and the railway, there was no room for expansion. The police found it hard to control daily crowds of up to 7,500 and traffic congestion was a growing issue. The search for a new ground became a priority.

Left: Tea on the lawns at Worple Road, 1906
Above from top to bottom: A Championship ticket, 1919;
Crowds watching the Singles' Challenge Round, 1880

Stars of Worple Road

GENTLEMEN

During the 1880s the twins **William** and **Ernest Renshaw** were the dominant players. Virtually unbeatable for a decade, they developed a unique style with strong serves, smashes and aggressive volleying which transformed the game. William was the more successful singles' player, winning the title seven times (including six in a row). **Wilfred Baddeley**, also successful in doubles with his brother Herbert, was the next major star and a three-time champion.

Brothers **Reginald** and **Laurence Doherty**, born in Wimbledon, were renowned for grace and sportsmanship as well as superb skill, lifting the game to new heights of popularity. They also advanced the game internationally. Reggie won the singles four times and younger brother Laurie five times. A later three-time winner was **Arthur Gore**.

By 1910, the field for The Championships was becoming increasingly international. Australian **Norman Brookes** became the first man from overseas to win the title in 1907. He was also the first left-hander. The charismatic New Zealander **Anthony Wilding** won the singles four times and became the idol of the crowds before sadly being killed in the First World War.

In 1920 and 1921 the mighty **Bill Tilden** won his first two Wimbledon titles (a third would be won at the new ground in 1930). The first American man to win the men's singles and a seven-time US title-holder, with a strong serve and masterful all-round game, 'Big Bill' is regarded as one of the great players of the game.

William Renshaw
1881, 1882, 1883, 1884,
1885, 1886, 1889

Ernest Renshaw
1888

Wilfred Baddeley
1891, 1892, 1895

Reginald and Laurence Doherty
Reginald: 1897, 1898, 1899, 1900
Laurence: 1902, 1903, 1904, 1905, 1906

Arthur Gore
1901, 1908, 1909

Norman Brookes
1907, 1914

Anthony Wilding
1910, 1911, 1912, 1913

Bill Tilden
1920, 1921, 1930

LADIES

Among the women, four players dominated the Ladies' Singles during the first three decades of The Championships. The first was **Blanche Bingley/Hillyard** who won six times in the period from 1886 to 1900. Born in Middlesex, she was one of the first ladies to serve overarm. Her reign was interrupted in 1887 by the extraordinary **Charlotte ('Lottie') Dod**, aged just 15 and still the youngest winner. Fast around the court and a good volleyer, Lottie was unbeaten in her five Championships before she successfully moved on to other sporting pursuits. Another five-time winner and rival of Blanche was the steady and determined **Charlotte Cooper/Sterry**.

The most successful player of the pre-war period was **Dorothea Douglass/Chambers**. A Middlesex-born vicar's daughter, tall and with a deadly forehand, she was a formidable competitor and won seven singles titles between 1903 and 1914. She enjoyed a great rivalry with American **May Sutton** who, in 1905, became the first overseas winner at Wimbledon.

Blanche Bingley/Hillyard
1886, 1889, 1894,
1897, 1899, 1900

Charlotte Dod
1887, 1888, 1891, 1892, 1893

Charlotte Cooper/Sterry
1895, 1896, 1898,
1901, 1908

Dorothea Douglass/Chambers
1903, 1904, 1906, 1910,
1911, 1913, 1914

May Sutton
1905, 1907

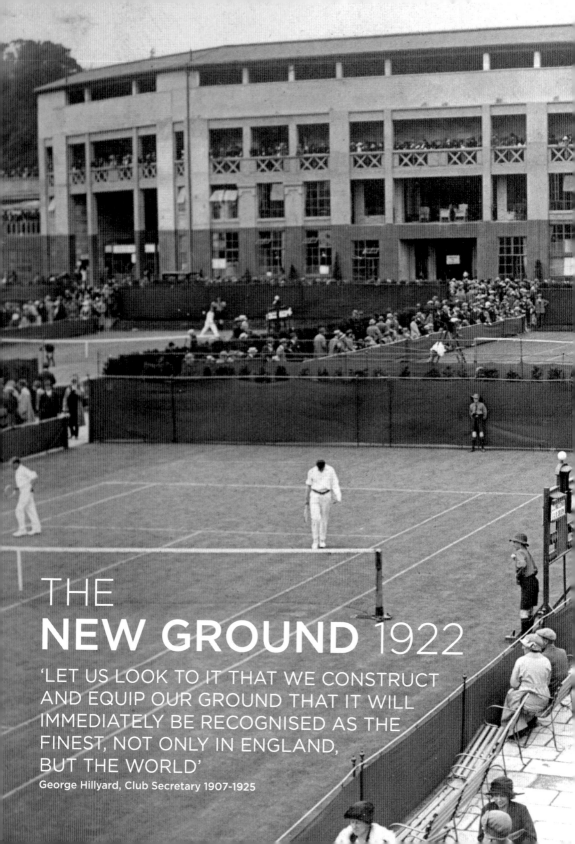

THE
NEW GROUND 1922

'LET US LOOK TO IT THAT WE CONSTRUCT
AND EQUIP OUR GROUND THAT IT WILL
IMMEDIATELY BE RECOGNISED AS THE
FINEST, NOT ONLY IN ENGLAND,
BUT THE WORLD'

George Hillyard, Club Secretary 1907-1925

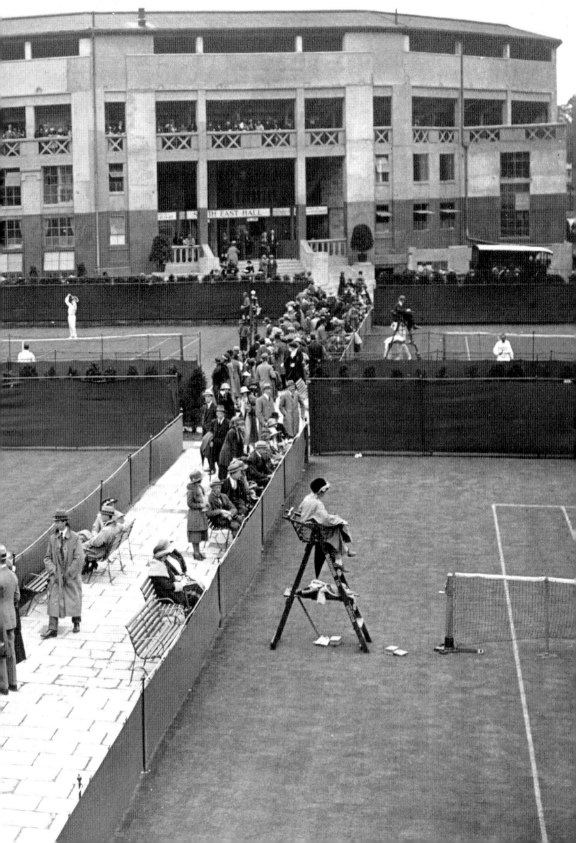

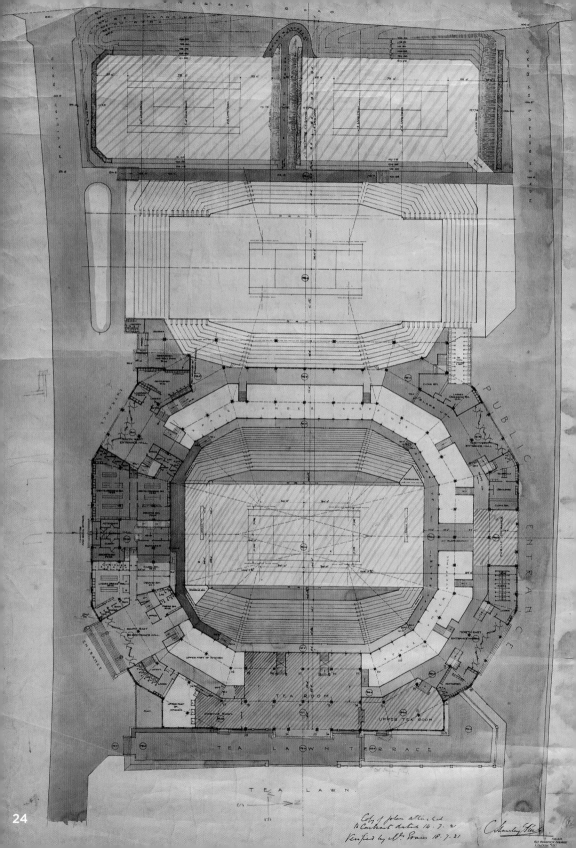

FARMLAND OPPOSITE WIMBLEDON PARK WAS IDENTIFIED AS A SUITABLE SITE FOR THE NEW GROUND.

A company was formed in 1920 to raise funds to buy the 13.5 acre site, situated just off what is now Church Road in Wimbledon.

The prominent architect Captain Stanley Peach was engaged to design a new 'Centre Court' (as the central court at Worple Road was also known). It would be the largest of its kind in the world. There would

also be 12 other courts, public catering areas and parking space for 400 vehicles. Turf was brought down from Cumberland in the north of England to provide the grass.

The new grounds and Centre Court were ready in time for the 1922 Championships. The opening ceremony was presided over by King George V, accompanied by Queen Mary. The tournament itself was probably the wettest on record. It rained on every day of the meeting and the last shots were not struck until the third Wednesday.

The Challenge Round was abolished, so that the previous year's champion now competed from the first round alongside all other competitors. The new Gentlemen's Champion was Australia's Gerald Patterson while Suzanne Lenglen of France defended successfully to win the fourth of her six singles titles.

The move to the new ground had proved successful. A new era for The Championships had begun.

STANLEY PEACH'S CENTRE COURT FEATURED:
9,989 seats across 3 miles of seating, 3,600 standing capacity, a tea room to seat 1,000 people, 47 staircases, 7 showers and 12 baths in the players' dressing rooms.

Previous page: The view of Courts 8 and 9 towards Centre Court, 1922
Left: Original Stanley Peach architectural plan, 1921
Above: Championship programme, 1922

GENTLEMEN

In the 1920s and 1930s, Wimbledon became increasingly international with leading French and American players bringing film star glamour to Wimbledon.

The leading French players – **Jean Borotra**, **René Lacoste**, **Henri Cochet** and Jacques 'Toto' Brugnon – were known as the Four Musketeers and added Gallic style and charm to the 1920s. The powerful Californian **Don Budge** was a triple champion at Wimbledon in 1937 and 1938 winning the singles, doubles and mixed titles. In 1938 he also became the first player to hold all four Grand Slam singles titles at the same time, after which he turned professional.

Fred Perry became the toast of Britain with his trio of Championship victories in 1934, 1935 and 1936. His determination, style and attacking forehand enabled him to win not only these titles but also the championships of the US, Australia and France (the first player to complete a 'career' Grand Slam). He also led Britain to four consecutive Davis Cup victories and was by far the most successful British men's player of the century.

Jean Borotra
1924, 1926

René Lacoste
1925, 1928

Henri Cochet
1927, 1929

Fred Perry
1934, 1935, 1936

Don Budge
1937, 1938

LADIES

After a successful three-year reign as champion at Worple Road, the glamorous Frenchwoman **Suzanne Lenglen** dominated ladies' tennis in the 1920s. She became triple champion three times, winning the singles, doubles and mixed in the same year. Just as invincible was her successor, Californian **Helen Wills/Moody**. Her record of eight singles' titles at Wimbledon would stand for more than 50 years. Her only defeat was in 1924, her first year, when she was beaten in the final by Britain's **Kitty McKane/Godfree**, who also won a second title two years later.

Another British winner was **Dorothy Round** with two titles in the 1930s, one in 1934 to complete a 'double' triumph for Britain in the singles alongside Fred Perry.

Other notable players of the 1930s included Americans **Helen Jacobs** and **Alice Marble**.

Suzanne Lenglen
1919, 1920, 1921,
1922, 1923, 1925

Kitty McKane/Godfree
1924, 1926

Helen Wills/Moody
1927, 1928, 1929, 1930,
1932, 1933, 1935, 1938

Dorothy Round
1934, 1937

Helen Jacobs
1936

Alice Marble
1939

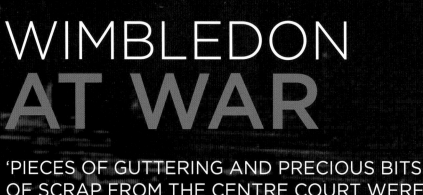

WIMBLEDON
AT WAR

'PIECES OF GUTTERING AND PRECIOUS BITS
OF SCRAP FROM THE CENTRE COURT WERE
USED IN THE BUILDING OF PIG STIES'

Norah Cleather, Club Secretary (Acting) 1939-1945

SIX CHAMPIONSHIPS WERE NOT PLAYED BECAUSE OF THE SECOND WORLD WAR.

On 31 August 1939, nursing staff, the Red Cross and the St John Ambulance Brigade moved in to the All England Club. The Fire Service, Air Raid Protection squads and the Civil Defence later took up residence, whilst the London Irish and the 1st Battalion of the Welsh Guards used the main concourse outside the Clubhouse as a parade ground. A decontamination unit was set up under Centre Court in case of a gas attack.

The Club did not escape bomb damage. A total of five bombs fell on the Grounds. On the night of Friday 11 October 1940 the perimeter roof of Centre Court was struck, demolishing 1,200 seats. The Championships resumed in 1946 but the damage was still apparent and ground capacity was limited. Many spectators were still in uniform.

CIVILIAN SERVICES and troops were not the only occupants of Wimbledon during the war. The car parks were ploughed up for vegetables and a farmyard was established with pigs, rabbits, chickens, ducks and geese – even a donkey.

Centre Court, 1940
Above: Club Secretary Norah Cleather and Marie Bompas (with racket) feeding the pigs, 1940

Stars
★ OF THE ★
1940s, 50s AND 60s
Gentlemen

The period after the Second World War saw a series of fine American players including, in the 1950s, **Jack Kramer** and **Tony Trabert** who became leading professional players.

There followed years of Australian leadership of the men's game – starting with the graceful, all-round strength of **Frank Sedgman** and reaching new heights of power and dynamism with the gifted **Lew Hoad** (twice a winner). Then came the red-headed, left-handed genius known as the 'Rockhampton Rocket'. **Rod Laver** won in 1961 and 1962 before turning professional, and then confirmed his status at the pinnacle of the game with further wins in 1968 and 1969 after Wimbledon became 'open' to professionals. In 1962 and 1969 Laver also won the full 'Grand Slam' of major championships in the same year – a feat, among the men, only previously achieved by American Don Budge in 1938.

Other Australian winners of the 'amateur' 1960s included the athletic **Roy Emerson** who won two Wimbledon singles titles, many doubles titles and numerous other victories worldwide. **John Newcombe**, with his resolute serve-and-volley game, was the last 'amateur' singles champion in 1967.

Jack Kramer
1947

Frank Sedgman
1952

Tony Trabert
1955

Lew Hoad
1956, 1957

Rod Laver
1961, 1962, 1968, 1969

Roy Emerson
1964, 1965

John Newcombe
1967, 1970, 1971

Stars

1940s, 50s AND 60s

Ladies

In the Ladies' Singles, Americans dominated Wimbledon after the war. **Louise Brough** stands out with her three successive victories from 1948 and a fourth in 1955. Her all-round skill led to numerous doubles titles and she was twice triple champion at Wimbledon.

In the early 1950s, **Maureen Connolly** ('Little Mo') used the accuracy and pace of her groundstrokes to win the title for three successive years, beginning in 1952 and aged just 17. A riding accident tragically ended her career before she turned 21. In the later 1950s, the tall and athletic **Althea Gibson** became the first black player to win the Wimbledon title. She won twice before turning professional in 1959.

The 1960s produced outstanding champions. The graceful **Maria Bueno** won three titles with a fluid, attacking game. Her great rival, **Margaret Smith/Court**, also won three singles titles at Wimbledon along with numerous doubles titles. The Australian's all-round power and athleticism led to an astonishing total of 24 Grand Slam singles titles. The third great player of this period was **Billie Jean King**. The ebullient American, a supreme volleyer, won three singles titles in the late 1960s, then another three in the following decade. A multiple champion around the world, she played a leading part in advancing the women's professional game.

British women's tennis enjoyed much success in the 1960s. **Angela Mortimer** took the title in 1961 in an all-British final against Christine Truman. In 1969 **Ann Jones** defeated Margaret Court in the semi-finals and Billie Jean King in the final.

Louise Brough
1948, 1949, 1950, 1955

Maureen Connolly
1952, 1953, 1954

Althea Gibson
1957, 1958

Maria Bueno
1959, 1960, 1964

Angela Mortimer
1961

Margaret Smith/Court
1963, 1965, 1970

Billie Jean King
1966, 1967, 1968,
1972, 1973, 1975

Ann Jones
1969

WIMBLEDON LEADS
'OPEN' TENNIS

'THE ONLY RESTRICTION ON ENTRY
WILL BE PLAYING ABILITY'

Herman David, AELTC Chairman, 1968

After the Second World War, all major tennis tournaments remained restricted to 'amateurs'. There was no prize money and no financial remuneration permitted for playing. Many fine American and Australian players, winners of titles at Wimbledon or elsewhere, chose to turn 'professional' and were lost to future Wimbledons.

Herman David, ex-Davis Cup player and chairman of The All England Lawn Tennis Club, with the support of the Lawn Tennis Association, worked tirelessly behind the scenes to achieve 'open' tennis and the end of 'shamateurism'. 'Shamateurism' was the practice of players receiving unofficial payments in amateur tournaments. In December 1967 Britain decided to go it alone by staging open tournaments in which professionals and amateurs would play side by side. The first open Wimbledon in 1968 combined nostalgia and high excitement. Rod Laver won the Gentlemen's Singles, picking up where he had left off as an amateur in 1962 and Billie Jean King won the Ladies' Singles.

Open tennis gave a fresh boost to the game. From the 1970s onwards, the leading players on the professional tours were athletes of great power and drive. Prize money became substantial and players attracted valuable endorsement contracts. Importantly, the very best players in the world could and did continue to compete for the supreme prize of a Wimbledon crown.

Above: A ticket for No.1 Court, 1968
Right: *The Daily Express* newspaper, 15 December, 1967

FRANK
ROSTRON reports

The motion is put:
"to delete all reference to
amateurs and professionals
from the rules" at yesterday's
Lawn Tennis Association
meeting. There were only five
dissentients. Spot one if you can.

IT'S ALL OPEN NOW

BRITISH lawn tennis will be "open" from April 22 next year. The shamateur was kicked out yesterday at the most momentous annual meeting in the Lawn Tennis Association's 80-year history.

Three hundred legislators, representing tennis clubs throughout the country, voted overwhelmingly to abolish the distinction between amateur and professional. Only five delegates voted against the proposal.

The first tournament to be played under the new regulations will be the British hard courts championships at Bournemouth, starting on April 22.

From then on, all British tennis, including Wimbledon, will be open with specific legal payments available to any players on merit.

'OUTLAWED' THREAT

Britain now stands in grave danger of being outlawed by the rest of world tennis, for the decision to go it alone was in defiance of the International Lawn Tennis Federation.

The only hope of saving British tennis from international "quarantine" is that the federation sub-committee, ordered to produce a solution to the dispute by mid-April, will grant each country the right of self-determination.

That was why the original motion for Britain to go it alone from January 1 next was dropped yesterday in favour of an amendment by Cecil Betts (Middlesex). He proposed that deletion of all reference to amateurs and professionals in the rules should be delayed until after the federation's meeting.

How do we play this shot now there are to be no backhanders?

STARS OF THE
1970s, 80s AND 90s
GENTLEMEN

Tennis moved into a new era and one player dominated the second half of the 1970s. Cool, fit and determined, **Björn Borg** won five successive Wimbledon singles titles. Although he was a six-time winner of the French title on clay, the Swede adapted to the faster grass with a fine serve and a double-fisted backhand that soon became widely adopted in the game. His final in 1980 against **John McEnroe**, with its dramatic fourth-set tie-break, ranks among the game's finest.

The American McEnroe went on to win three titles himself with his exquisite attacking talent – punctuated by infamous displays of temperament. Both Borg and McEnroe had many memorable battles with the American **Jimmy Connors**, who won the title twice. A third US player, **Arthur Ashe**, became the first black male singles champion in 1975, winning at the age of 31.

The power game moved to a new level with the arrival of **Boris Becker**. The German became the youngest Gentlemen's Singles Champion aged just 17 and unseeded when he won the first of this three titles in 1985 with hard all-round power. From 1987 three finals followed with his great rival, **Stefan Edberg** of Sweden. The elegant serve-and-volleying Swede won two of those finals to become a popular champion.

In the 1990s Wimbledon became the home of **Pete Sampras**. The American won the singles title seven times in eight years and his magnificent serve and stealthy speed of movement made him one of the game's finest ever grass court players. His most notable rival, winning the title in 1992, was fellow countryman **Andre Agassi**. His colourful fashion sense and charismatic personality made him a Wimbledon favourite.

Jimmy Connors
1974, 1982

Arthur Ashe
1975

Björn Borg
1976, 1977, 1978,
1979, 1980

John McEnroe
1981, 1983, 1984

Boris Becker
1985, 1986, 1989

Stefan Edberg
1988, 1990

Andre Agassi
1992

Pete Sampras
1993, 1994, 1995, 1997,
1998, 1999, 2000

STARS OF THE
1970s, 80s AND 90s

LADIES

Among the ladies, the Australian **Evonne Goolagong/Cawley** charmed the crowds with her joyful brilliance on court. She won her singles titles in 1971 and 1980. **Chris Evert/Lloyd** brought a game of shrewd and steady play together with a double-fisted backhand. She was Singles Champion at Wimbledon three times during a lengthy period at the top of the game, always enjoying wide support. Britain's **Virginia Wade** had a fine victory over Betty Stove in the 1977 final to become Champion in the year of Wimbledon's centenary and the Queen's Silver Jubilee.

The reign of **Martina Navratilova** began in 1978. The Czech-born left-hander took the women's game to new levels of fitness and power and she became the most successful tennis player ever at Wimbledon. She won the singles a record nine times, including a run of six consecutive years in the 1980s, along with 11 Ladies' and Mixed Doubles titles.

Her successor as the dominant woman player was **Steffi Graf**. The athletic German with a supreme forehand won the Wimbledon title seven times over a nine-year period, beginning with an epoch-changing win over Navratilova in 1988. This was also the year in which Graf won all four Grand Slam singles titles as well as the newly-restored Olympic title. Her last victory was in 1996. In 1997 a 16-year-old **Martina Hingis** became the youngest champion since Lottie Dod a century earlier.

Evonne Goolagong/Cawley
1971, 1980

Chris Evert/Lloyd
1974, 1976, 1981

Virginia Wade
1977

Martina Navratilova
1978, 1979, 1982, 1983, 1984,
1985, 1986, 1987, 1990

Steffi Graf
1988, 1989, 1991, 1992,
1993, 1995, 1996

Martina Hingis
1997

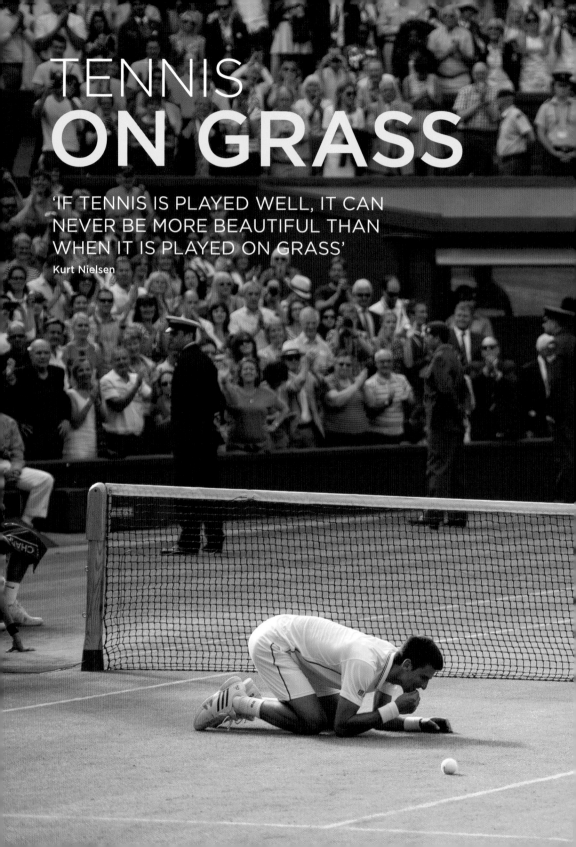

TENNIS
ON GRASS

'IF TENNIS IS PLAYED WELL, IT CAN
NEVER BE MORE BEAUTIFUL THAN
WHEN IT IS PLAYED ON GRASS'

Kurt Nielsen

WIMBLEDON'S GRASS SURFACE IS THE TOURNAMENT'S MOST DISTINCTIVE FEATURE.

The Championships at Wimbledon is now the only Grand Slam event played on grass.

Two inventions in the 19th century were essential to lawn tennis. First was the lawn mower, invented by Edwin Budding in 1830. Without its arrival to replace the scythe, grass could never have been cut short enough to allow a tennis ball to bounce accurately. Equally important was Charles Goodyear's discovery in 1839 of how to vulcanise rubber. It became possible to make pressurised balls that would bounce high enough on a well-rolled lawn.

In 1870 a gardener was engaged by the All England Club at a wage of four shillings a day. Gardeners continued to maintain the croquet lawns and tennis courts until 1888 when a Head Groundsman was appointed. This role has been vital ever since. A year-round programme of rigorous care and maintenance is involved, including removal of any thatch, over-sowing with perennial rye grass seed, mowing, watering, more over-sowing, rolling and cutting to a height of 8mm prior to the tournament. The hardness of the soil, crucial to the bounce of the ball, is constantly tested. The highest-quality playing surface must be produced for the world's best players to display their full range of shots.

Previous page: Novak Djokovic eating grass on Centre Court, 2014
Above from top to bottom: Ransome's Lawn Mower advert, 1880s; London Transport panel poster by Herry Perry, 1931; Handmower by Ransome and Sims of Ipswich, 1855
Right: Groundsmen preparing Centre Court, 1931

BALL BOYS AND GIRLS, POISED AND IN UNIFORM, ARE ONE OF WIMBLEDON'S TRADITIONAL SIGHTS.

In the 1920s and 1930s, ball boys were provided by the Shaftesbury Homes charity. From 1946, they were volunteers from local schools and institutions including Barnardo's Homes. Ball girls were first introduced at Wimbledon in 1977. Around 250 boys and girls are now selected from local schools and they receive intensive training (often on Wimbledon's indoor courts) from February onwards until The Championships. During the tournament, the ball boys and girls work in teams of six.

WHAT MAKES A BALL BOY OR GIRL?

Between 14-16
The average age is 15

Determined
Only 250 are selected from more than 700 applicants from local schools

Prepared to work hard
Weekly training starts in February

Fit, enthusiastic and capable of standing out
Training sessions last for 2-2.5 hours with 50-60 young people

Have plenty of stamina
Ball boys and girls work one hour on, one hour off

Organised
Six teams of six look after Centre Court and No.1 Court, six teams look after the other show courts, the 30 remaining teams rotate between all the courts

Left: Official ball boys and girls photo, 2013
Above from left to right: Ball girls were introduced, 1977; Ball boys ready for action, 2013

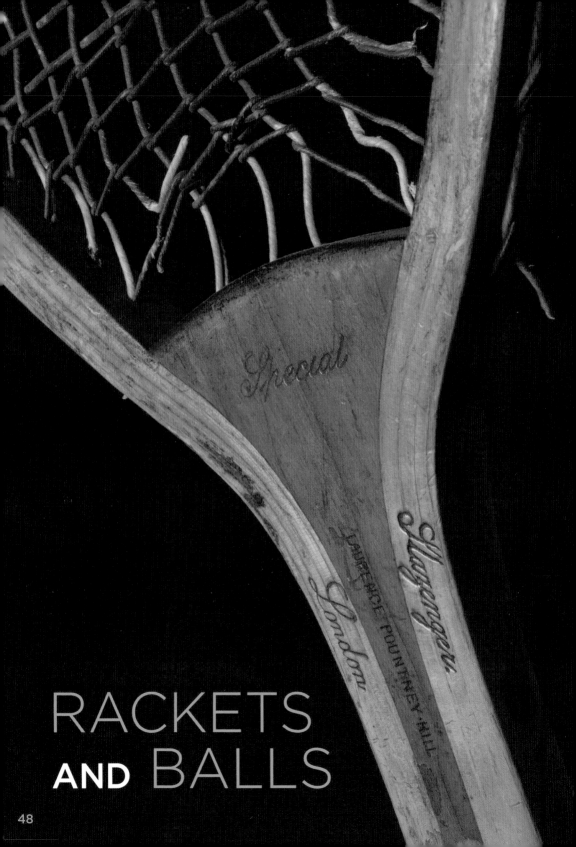

RACKETS
AND BALLS

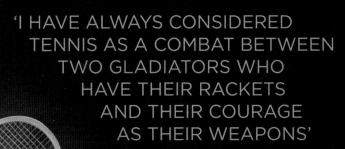

'I HAVE ALWAYS CONSIDERED
TENNIS AS A COMBAT BETWEEN
TWO GLADIATORS WHO
HAVE THEIR RACKETS
AND THEIR COURAGE
AS THEIR WEAPONS'

Yannick Noah

Craftsmen and inventors have experimented with racket design since the game began. Early rackets with slightly curved heads were direct descendants of real tennis rackets. They were made from single pieces of ash and handles were grooved to improve grip. By the 1880s racket heads had become symmetrical, shoulders were taped for extra strength and the tension of the gut strings was increased. The invention of lamination – the gluing together of several thin strips of wood to form the frame – opened new horizons. Rackets, incorporating other woods like beech and hickory and even thin strips of fibre, could now be made lighter and stronger.

Left: Slazenger EGM racket used by Reggie Doherty, c1895
Above: Display of wooden rackets in the Museum

MAJOR CHANGES BEGAN WHEN RACKETS MADE OF STEEL AND ALUMINIUM, SOME INCORPORATING FIBREGLASS, CAME ONTO THE MARKET.

In 1968 Billie Jean King became the first Wimbledon singles' champion to use a metal racket. By 1988, there were no players using wooden rackets.

Today's lightweight frames made of modern materials such as graphite, boron and titanium, with larger heads and new types of stringing, have transformed the style of play. Virtually all today's players, men and women, now play with ever-increasing topspin and with the ability to reach and play shots previously not feasible.

AS FOR THE BALLS, THOSE FIRST USED AT WIMBLEDON HAD FLANNEL COVERS SEWN BY HAND.

Covers with white cloth or melton, a type of heavy woollen cloth, then became increasingly popular. In 1880 F. H. Ayres began providing balls for Wimbledon. In 1902 Slazenger took over the contract and has been supplying The Championships ever since. Innovation has been constant: stitched seams gave way to vulcanised seams and, in the 1950s, nylon-reinforced covers prolonged playing life. In 1986 yellow balls were introduced to improve visibility. Boris Becker and Martina Navratilova are the only players to win singles' titles at Wimbledon playing with both white and yellow balls. More recently, even higher visibility wet-weather finishes have come into play. The weight, size, bounce and compression of balls are all tightly regulated for the Grand Slam tournaments.

White Slazenger ball, 1922   White Slazenger ball, 1937   Wartime uncovered ball   Yellow Slazenger ball, 1980s

SLAZENGER has been supplying tennis balls to The Championships since 1902.

Various innovations, including vulcanised seams and nylon felt, make sure that the best players in the world have the best equipment.

THE ROYAL
CONNECTION

'AT WIMBLEDON THINGS COME TO A PITCH.
THE BEST GRASS. THE BEST CROWD. THE
ROYALTY. YOU PLAY YOUR BEST TENNIS'

Rod Laver

IN 1907 THE PRINCE OF WALES VISITED WIMBLEDON AT THE INVITATION OF CLUB SECRETARY GEORGE HILLYARD.

Since the Prince's visit, accompanied by Princess Mary, there has been a strong association with Britain's Royal Family. The Prince became the Club's President and then later its Patron on his accession to the throne as George V – a position maintained by succeeding monarchs.

King George V and Queen Mary were avid spectators and attended The Championships most years from 1919 to 1934. After the King's death, Queen Mary continued to attend. In the Jubilee Championships of 1926, their son, the

Duke of York (later King George VI), played in the Gentlemen's Doubles event, losing in the first round.

The long and proud association with the Kent family began in 1929 when Prince George became President of the Club. Following his death in 1942, his widow continued as President, first as the Duchess of Kent and from 1961 as Princess Marina. Since 1969, the present Duke has carried out his duties as President with great enthusiasm.

In 1977, the year of her Silver Jubilee and her third visit to The Championships, Her Majesty The Queen witnessed Virginia Wade's emotional win over Betty Stove before presenting the trophies. Other members of the Royal Family also attend frequently.

The Royal Box, at the south end of Centre Court, seats 74 people. In addition to members of the Royal Family, it is used to entertain invited guests from the tennis world and prominent individuals from other walks of life.

Left: Virginia Wade collects the Ladies' trophy from HM The Queen, 1977
Top to bottom: The Duke of York playing in the Gentlemen's Doubles, 1926;
The Duke and Duchess of Cambridge in the Royal Box, 2014
Above right: Official programme for the Jubilee Championships, 1926

PREDOMINANTLY
IN WHITE

'TENNIS WHITES ARE BORING. UNLESS IT'S AT WIMBLEDON WHERE IT'S CLASSY'
Serena Williams

A unique feature of Wimbledon is the players' white clothing, striking against the green grass. It was the ladies of the 1880s who, wishing to avoid any signs of perspiration, first established the convention of all-white clothes – there was no specific rule. Their multi-layered outfits, illustrated opposite, gave no concession to physical exercise and weighed as much as 4.9kg. Long garments, restrictive corsets and heavy layers of petticoats for ladies in the 19th century gave way after the First World War to a more liberated era.

WHILE WOMEN'S TENNIS WEAR WAS RADICALLY OVERHAULED, for men the change was less profound. Victorian men wore cream or white, often with coloured sash belts and ties. Long, comfortable trousers remained popular well into the new century. In 1927 a crocodile symbol was designed for the dashing French player René Lacoste, whose elegant blazer by Motsch & Fils can be seen in the Museum. In 1933 Britain's Bunny Austin was the first player to wear shorts on Centre Court.

Above from left to right: René Lacoste at Wimbledon, 1926; Bunny Austin wearing shorts, 1933

A VICTORIAN LADY
DRESSES FOR TENNIS

Petticoat to go over
undergarment

Corset, to go over
undergarment

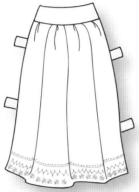

Second petticoat to go over first
petticoat (and sometimes a third
petticoat and bustle as well)

A tennis player in
her undergarments

Straw boater

Black leather shoes with
rubberised soles

Dress, made of fine
wool or silk

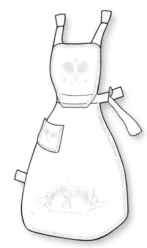

Tennis apron, to go over dress

FASHION
THROUGH THE YEARS

Cotton piqué tennis dress with a divided skirt, c1932

Polyester tennis dress with a purple hem worn by Mary Hardwick Hare, 1958, similar to one worn by Maria Bueno

Cotton piqué tennis dress with v neck and dropped waist, mid-1920s

Suzanne Lenglen transformed women's tennis fashion with her knee-length cotton dresses and short sleeves. Freedom of movement and style later led to bare legs and ankle socks.

After the Second World War, the creations of designer Ted Tinling caused admiration – and controversy. It was his 'shocking' use of colour on designs for Maria Bueno that led to the entry conditions for The Championships in 1963 stating for the first time that competitors must be dressed 'predominantly in white'. In 1995 this was clarified further to require that each item of clothing must be 'almost entirely white'. In 2014, this was extended to include shoes, visible underwear and accessories such as caps and wristbands.

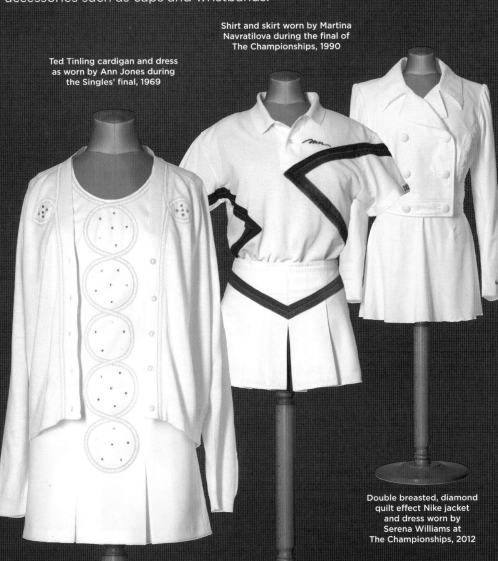

Shirt and skirt worn by Martina Navratilova during the final of The Championships, 1990

Ted Tinling cardigan and dress as worn by Ann Jones during the Singles' final, 1969

Double breasted, diamond quilt effect Nike jacket and dress worn by Serena Williams at The Championships, 2012

THE CHAMPIONSHIP
TROPHIES

MISS HILL JACOBS. MISS D.E. ROUND. 1937. M

MISS D.E. ROUND. MRS F.S. MOODY. MISS S. PRY. 1956. MISS L. BROUGH.

1934

MISS D.E. ROUND. MISS M. C. SMOODY. 1955. M

H.M. MISS M. HINDLEY.

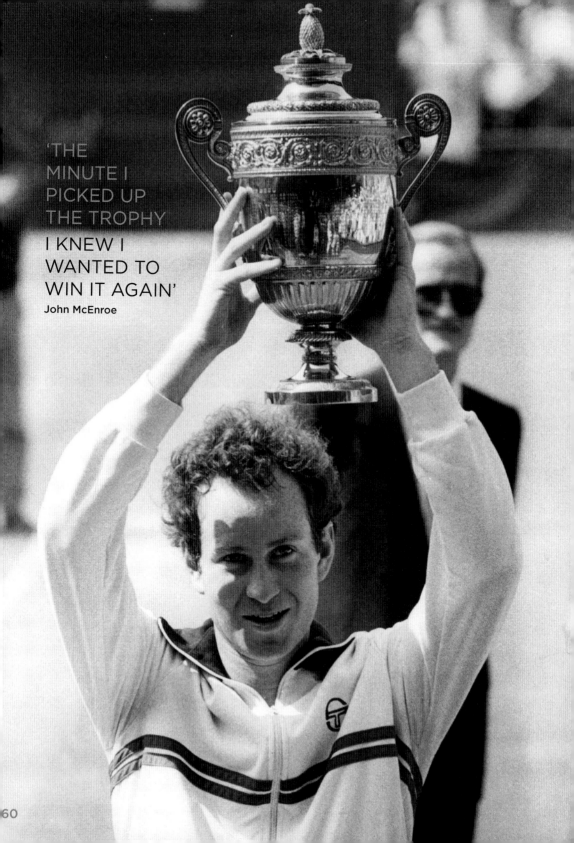

'THE MINUTE I PICKED UP THE TROPHY

I KNEW I WANTED TO WIN IT AGAIN'
John McEnroe

THE CHAMPIONSHIP TROPHIES ARE AMONG THE MOST POPULAR EXHIBITS IN THE MUSEUM.

The original Gentlemen's Singles trophy was the Field Cup, donated by *The Field* newspaper for the inaugural Championship in 1877. William Renshaw's victories in three successive years in 1881-83 allowed him to keep the trophy. His further three victories in 1884-86 also entitled him to the replacement Challenge Cup. The new Challenge Cup, bought in 1887 at a cost of 100 guineas and inscribed for the 'Single-Handed Championship of the World', is presented each year to the singles champion but now never leaves the Grounds. With no more space left on the Cup by 2009 to engrave the names of the winners, an ebonised wooden plinth with an ornamental silver gilt band was designed to accompany the Cup and now bears the latest winners' names.

The Ladies' Singles trophy dates from 1886. It is a magnificent partly-gilded silver salver known as the 'Rosewater Dish' or the 'Venus Rosewater Dish'. It is called Venus because of the goddess images on the trophy. The trophy bears no inscription other than engraving of the dates and names of the champions. Names began on the inside of the salver but from 1958 they have been on the reverse side.

In 1949 Ted Schroeder was the first winner to be presented with a trophy on Centre Court itself. He was presented with the President's Cup, now a retired trophy. This was given to the men's singles champion on court until 1968. Since then the Challenge Cup has been presented.

The presentation ceremony has since become a traditional part of proceedings on finals days. No prize money is handed out on court but is collected later. One tradition is that, by the time the ceremony for each singles event has ended and the players return into the entrance hall of the Clubhouse, the honours board already records the name of the latest champion.

Since 1987 the runners-up in the singles' events have received a silver salver. It is also the custom for the singles winners to receive a three-quarters size replica of the trophy they have won.

Left: McEnroe holds the Gentlemen's Singles trophy, 1984
This page from top to bottom: Serena Williams with the Ladies' Singles trophy, 2009; Ted Schroeder with the President's Cup, 1949

WIMBLEDON
IN THE 21st CENTURY

'THEY ACT LIKE THEY'VE GOT THE BIGGEST
TOURNAMENT IN THE WORLD. THEY DO.
THIS IS THE BIG ONE'
Pete Sampras

WIMBLEDON ENTERED THE 21ST CENTURY WITH ITS REPUTATION AND POPULARITY AS HIGH AS EVER.

The game of tennis is truly global. Great players, of all nationalities around the world, compete for the sport's most prestigious title.

The Grounds continue to develop to meet the needs of The Championships, as tradition merges with innovation. A long-term plan began in 1994 with the building of a new No.1 Court seating 11,500 spectators. The Millennium Building opened in 2000 with new facilities for players, media, officials and members. New No.2 and No.3 Courts were built for the 2009 and 2011 Championships respectively. The computerised Player Challenge System ('Hawk-Eye') for reviewing controversial line decisions came into operation in 2007.

Perhaps the most significant change so far this century has been the new retractable roof over Centre Court. Completed in 2009, it enables play to continue even in inclement weather or if play is delayed into the evening. When the roof is closing, supporting roof trusses move apart like a concertina and stretch a translucent fabric over the court. An air-management system operates to enable safe play on grass. When closed, a new atmosphere is created on the world's most famous court.

From 2015 The Championships started one week later than previously, extending the period after the end of the French Open to three weeks. This allows players to recover and prepare better for Wimbledon's grass.

Plans are underway for future building developments. Most notably, a retractable roof will be provided for No.1 Court. Other improvements are continually being considered. Wimbledon does not, and cannot, remain unchanged as it maintains its position as the finest stage in world tennis.

Left: Roger Federer under the Centre Court roof, 2014
Above top to bottom: The Player Challenge System, 2013;
Digital rendition of the AELTC Master Plan created by Grimshaw Architects

STARS OF THE

2000s AND 2010s

GENTLEMEN

The opening decade or so of the 21st century has seen players and matches as memorable as any in the game's history. For drama, few finals equal that in 2001 when Croatia's **Goran Ivanisevic** became the only 'wild card' to win a Grand Slam singles title in a pulsating final delayed by rain until the third Monday.

In 2003 the reign of Switzerland's **Roger Federer** began. Setting new records, his majestic play and graceful style have been unsurpassed. With six Wimbledon titles in the 2000s, his seventh title in 2012 equalled the record of William Renshaw and Pete Sampras. His great rival became clay court specialist **Rafael Nadal**. The Spanish left-hander's intensity of play made him a powerful force. His victory in 2008 over Federer, after nearly five hours and ending in the evening dusk, ranks among the most memorable Wimbledon finals. A third great player with the strength of his all-round play is **Novak Djokovic**. The Serbian's dramatic five-set final win against Federer in 2014 is another that will last in the memory. **Andy Murray** became the first British Gentlemen's Singles Champion at Wimbledon for 77 years in 2013.

LADIES

Amongst the women, the opening decade of the new century belonged to the extraordinary sisters **Venus** and **Serena Williams**. At least one Williams sister played in every Wimbledon Ladies' final of the 2000s (except 2006) and they played each other four times. Between them they won eight singles titles in that period (five to Venus) with Serena, the younger sister, continuing her multiple title victories into the following decade. Together, they also won the doubles five times. They have taken the women's game to new levels of accomplishment. Serena Williams maintained her form into the 2010s and, with two successes in 2011 and 2014, the powerful Czech player **Petra Kvitova** asserted herself as a force to be reckoned with.

Venus Williams
2000, 2001, 2005,
2007, 2008

Goran Ivanisevic
2001

Serena Williams
2002, 2003, 2009,
2010, 2012

Roger Federer
2003, 2004, 2005, 2006,
2007, 2009, 2012

Rafael Nadal
2008, 2010

Novak Djokovic
2011, 2014

Petra Kvitova
2011, 2014

Andy Murray
2013

OLYMPIC
TENNIS

IN 2012 WIMBLEDON WAS PROUD TO HOST OLYMPIC TENNIS FOR A SECOND TIME.

It was a welcome return to Wimbledon after 104 years. In 1908 the outdoor Olympic event was staged on grass at the All England Club's Worple Road grounds and Britain won gold medals in both the men's and ladies' singles through **Major Ritchie** and **Dorothea Chambers**.

The scene in 2012 was very different from The Championships held just weeks earlier. Magenta-coloured canvas backgrounds were adorned with the five rings of the Olympics and the logo of the London Organising Committee who, with the International Tennis Federation, organised the event. The players wore coloured clothing instead of the traditional Wimbledon white.

The gold medal in the men's singles was again won by Britain with **Andy Murray** defeating Roger Federer in three straight sets. The ladies' gold medal was won by USA's **Serena Williams** whose victory was as accomplished as at The Championships the month before.

Left: Spectators watch a match outside the Clubhouse
Above from left to right: Major Ritchie and Dorothea Chambers, gold medallists, 1908;
Andy Murray and Serena Williams, gold medallists, 2012; Olympic Games programme, 1908

THE MUSEUM
AND THE TOUR

'WHEN I FIRST WALKED AROUND THE MUSEUM,
IT STILL CAME AS A SURPRISE TO DISCOVER
SUCH A DIVERSE COLLECTION OF PAINTINGS,
PHOTOGRAPHS, RACKETS, CLOTHING AND
GENERAL MEMORABILIA... THE MUSEUM
HAS SO MUCH TO OFFER'
John McEnroe

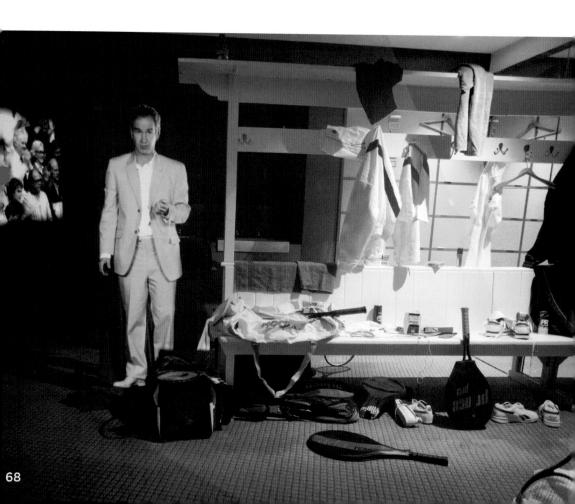

WIMBLEDON LAWN TENNIS MUSEUM HAS A COLLECTION OF MORE THAN 20,000 TENNIS-RELATED OBJECTS, REFLECTING THE HISTORY OF THE GAME FROM ITS EARLIEST BEGINNINGS TO THE PRESENT DAY.

The Museum is committed to keeping its collections up-to-date, ensuring new players' outfits, equipment and memorabilia are added each year at The Championships. Purpose-built environmentally controlled storage keeps the objects safe when they are not on display and items from the store regularly feature in special exhibitions and when changes are made in the Museum.

Left: John McEnroe's 'ghost' in the Gentlemen's changing room
Above from top to bottom, left to right: Rafael Nadal visits the Museum, 2010; 21st Century Modern Players showcase; Tennis Today display; Racket-maker's workshop re-created in the Museum

A VISIT TO WIMBLEDON LAWN TENNIS MUSEUM EVOKES A MAGICAL SENSE OF HISTORY AND TRADITION.

One of the attractions of a trip during most of the year is the opportunity to enjoy a behind-the-scenes guided tour of the Grounds. Memories are revived of the great champions and great matches that have graced the famous grass courts.

Work quietly goes on year-round to prepare for the next Championships and the tour gives visitors an ideal opportunity to see the facilities used by players and officials. As work is ongoing the tour route varies, however, sights and places commonly included on the tour include:

- AORANGI TERRACE
  Known to most as 'Henman Hill' – triggering memories of days with thousands of spectators picnicking and watching the action on the big screen; the Water Gardens at the top of the Terrace provide a calming environment as well as stunning views over London.

- COURT 18
  Where the longest match in the history of tournament tennis was played. Over a period of three days in the first week of the 2010 Championships, John Isner finally beat Nicolas Mahut (6-4, 3-6, 6-7, 7-6, 70-68) and a plaque now records the occasion.

- THE MILLENNIUM BUILDING
  With the Main Interview Room where the world's best tennis players are interviewed after their matches. Plus the player's entrance and other normally private facilities, as well as views of the southern area of the grounds.

- CENTRE COURT
  A magnificent view of the world's most famous tennis court, providing an emotional and unparalleled experience for all tennis fans.

Above from top to bottom: Aorangi Terrace, 2013; John Isner and Nicolas Mahut at the end of their record match, 2010; Roger Federer in the Main Interview Room, 2014; Centre Court Right: View over the Grounds, 2013.

WIMBLEDON LAWN TENNIS MUSEUM WILL CONTINUE TO REFLECT THE TRADITION, INNOVATION AND MAGIC OF THE CHAMPIONSHIPS.

THE KENNETH RITCHIE WIMBLEDON LIBRARY

The Library, part of the Museum, contains the world's most outstanding collection of British and foreign lawn tennis books, annuals, periodicals, programmes, newspaper cuttings, videos and DVDs. It is available to the general public for study and research.

The Library is open year round Monday to Friday 10am – 5pm but closed to the public during The Championships. Admission is by appointment only. Please call **+44 (0)20 8879 5609**.

LEARNING

Wimbledon Lawn Tennis Museum has a well-established Learning department catering for all age groups and abilities, from first time to later life learners. Participants are offered the opportunity to learn through a wide range of subjects and activities designed to open up the world of Wimbledon and engage all with the fascinating story of lawn tennis.

The Learning programme, which began in 2001, caters for over 6,000 students a year. Leaders can choose from workshops, lectures and guided tours of the grounds.

For further information, please visit **www.wimbledon.com/learning**